MW01593903

The Greater Understanding

Written & Illustrated by

Nanna Pete

Magpie Press

In a small country town, out in the middle of somewhere you may have heard of, there once lived a farmer.

This man wasn't just a farmer. He had a beautiful little family, whom he much adored. He was a loving father to his four children and a sweet husband to his wife. His family was extremely important to him.

The farmer was quiet and soft spoken. When the man did speak, he was always worth listening to. He was also good and kind to everyone.

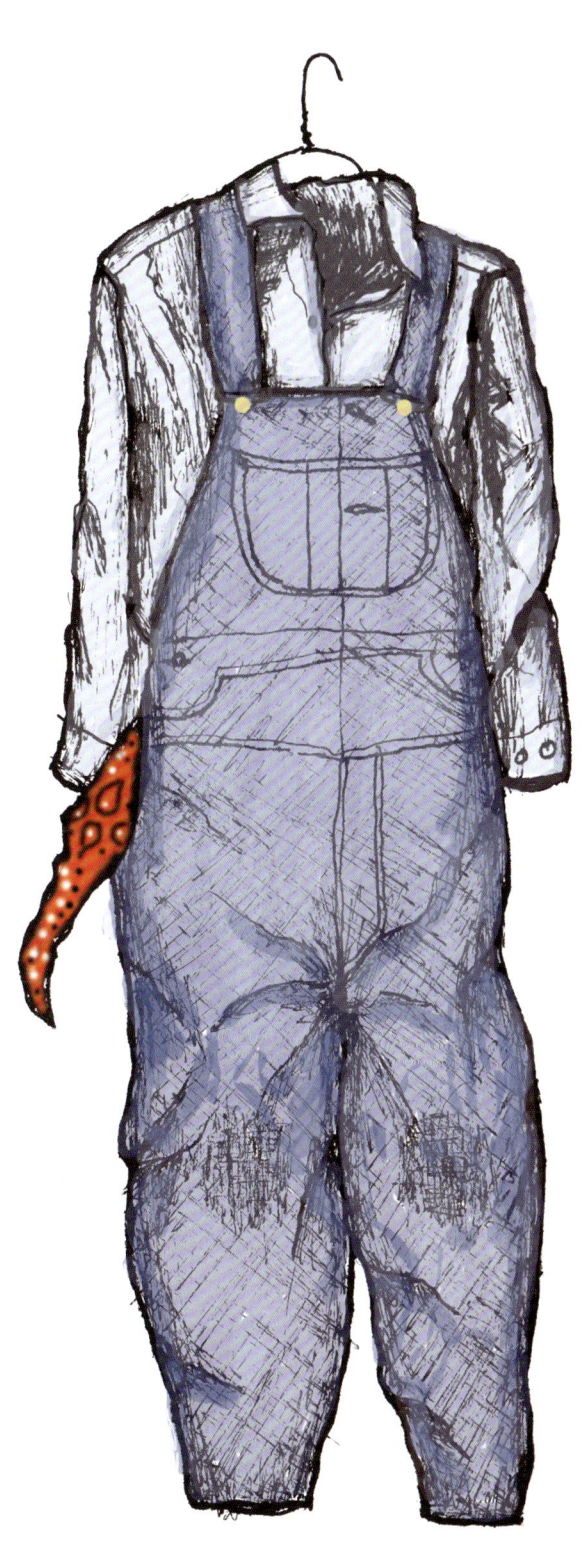

The farmer carried a red bandana handkerchief with him everywhere he went to help take care of his large, moist nose.

To work each day, he wore faded blue overalls, a long-sleeved button-front shirt, a large straw hat, and a pair of uncommonly large, well-worn brown leather work boots.

When asked, he would smile and jokingly say that his big feet gave him a greater understanding.

He loved the rich, earthen soil that he tended, as well as all of the glorious bounties his family enjoyed from his labors on the farm. He always made sure he rotated the crops properly to keep the soil strong and healthy.

The farmer pruned and cared for the fruit trees as well as the berry bushes and the grape vines that were tucked here and there all over the farm. This made the best use of every square inch of ground.

Corn and various grains were usually his cash crops and were also food for all the animals he cared for. The farmer chose the cash crops each year with great care. He and his family depended heavily on those crops for most of their yearly income.

Yesiree, the farmer loved his farm so very much.

However, he constantly battled the magpies, raccoons, and skunks that came along with the farm. They ate the chicken and duck eggs as well as the baby chicks and ducklings. He had a very healthy dislike for those creatures and did all he could to protect his feathered fowl friends from harm.

The farmer planted a tulip bed under one of his apple trees in his backyard and a row of irises right outside the back door so he could enjoy them.

In the springtime, he would bring fresh flowers into the house so his family could enjoy them inside as well as out. They loved the beautiful scents and colors.

The farmer had cows, chickens, ducks, and geese.

His fine feathered friends made a lot
of noise, and their commotion started
very, very early each morning.

The farmer's pride and joy was his VERY large vegetable garden. It was plumb full of every kind of vegetable that would grow in the local climate. This massively huge garden was used to feed his family all year long.

As his family grew, his children learned about hard work and responsibility while helping on the farm. Farm work brought his family together. They seemed to love each other a little more than most families.

The whole family was involved in harvesting, freezing, and canning the fruits and veggies to eat year round. He always raised more than he needed, just in case.

In the small town where the farmer lived, there were widows and families who struggled to feed everyone in their household.

The farmer was very aware of his neighbor's needs. He'd had many hungry days as a child and wanted to help others of all ages avoid the misery of starvation.

In the spring each year, little widow ladies in town would find large bunches of tulips and other flowers wrapped in newspaper and laid at their front door. The little widow ladies loved the flowers a lot.

They had no idea where they came from. There was no trace of anyone around, but there were some very large footprints in the dirt pathway leading to their door.

In the fall, struggling families and the widow ladies would find large bags of potatoes, corn, and other vegetables and fruits next to their front door. The food-filled bags kept many people from going hungry for several months of the year.

There was no trace of who brought them, except for the footprints in the dirt by their front door. Sometimes there was a set of smaller footprints alongside the big footprints.

In the winter, those who could not shovel their snow would wake to shoveled walks and driveways with no one in sight. All they could see were big boot prints sprinkled here and there in the snow. All of this continued for many years.

There were some hard times for the people in the town, but few ever went hungry.

No one ever spoke about that. They were all just so very grateful for what was freely, kindly, and secretly given.

The farmer's family had struggles too, but they had a good life together and worked hard every year to keep the farm going. Some years were easier than others, but things always worked out. The farmer cherished his family more than he ever imagined he could. His understanding and compassion for others also increased with the passing years.

Over time and increasing age, the farmer's children grew up and left home, and the farm became more difficult for the farmer to maintain by himself. But one year was the most difficult of all.

The farmer had been very healthy his whole life, but in one of his older years, he became very ill toward the end of summer, when he normally would have been harvesting his crops.

The doctor told the farmer's wife that he was quite worried about the farmer. The farmer had a high temperature and a very bad cough. He could hardly breathe.

The farmer's wife did her best to take care of him so he would get better. She worried about him a lot. She had also grown weaker with age. She couldn't help him much with the farm anymore, but she did her best to nurse him back to health.

The only thing the sick old farmer could do was lie in bed, which he disliked. He had spent most of his life working from dawn until dusk. He wanted to keep working, but he just couldn't do it. Instead, he slept most of the day and night for over a week.

Just when he felt like getting out of bed a bit, a huge storm passed over and brought heavy winds and rain for several days. That was always a very bad thing at harvest time. Most crops are laid flat on the ground by that kind of weather, and it makes harvesting most crops impossible.

The farmer was so worried, it made him feel sick again, and he went back to bed for a few more days. Neither he nor his wife could do anything but stay in the house.

The weather finally cleared and the farmer started feeling a bit better. He decided to go outside and survey the damage to his crops, especially the corn, which was their cash crop for that year.

When he went outside, he felt worse again as he looked around at his yard. His hopes sank when he saw the many fallen branches, leaves, and garbage everywhere.

He shook his head and started walking out to the corn fields. As he got closer to the fields, he saw that something was very different, but from a distance he couldn't figure out what he was seeing.

When he arrived at the edge of the corn fields, things became very clear. His corn fields had been completely laid down by the big storm and the stalks were lying flattened in the mud.

But much to his surprise, there were huge piles of corn cobs throughout his fields. He realized immediately that someone had hand-harvested his corn and saved the crop that would support him and his wife for the next year.

He looked around for any clues that would tell him who would have done this very hard job. It would have taken an army to perform such a task.

The only thing he could see were footprints of all sizes and shapes in the mud of the field and tire tracks from many different vehicles.

He then bowed his head, closed his eyes. And as tears ran down his cheeks, he dropped to his knees.

Indeed, he felt the deepest gratitude he had ever felt in his entire life.

The farmer is gone now and greatly missed,
but his kind acts will never be forgotten.
For it was on that day, in the corn field,
that the farmer discovered he truly did
have the greater understanding . . .

This greater understanding comes from
doing for others with never an expectation
of receiving anything in return. In his time
of great need, to have such a large service
performed was overwhelming, but even more
so to someone who had served so many and
never expected or asked anything from anyone.

That is a truly wonderful gift, to give so
much and then to learn how to receive
with grace and endless gratitude.

The Farmer

He was born and raised on a small farm in the Midwest. His parents were Swedish immigrants, and the farmer was number seven of ten children. They made their own clothes and shoes and cut their own hair. They grew their own food, both animals and plants.

He graduated from high school and put himself through college, graduating with a PhD in food chemistry. The farmer was a revered professor at a major university until he retired. For forty years, he would come home from work, take off his suit and put on his overalls. Off to work he went each evening, until the sun went down.

He bought the family farm from his dad while working through graduate school. He farmed it, raised his family there and lived on that farm he dearly loved until he died at the age of eighty-three and a half years.

Nanna Pete's Honey Vanilla Banana Cake

(the Farmer's daughter)

Ingredients:

7 large ripe bananas
4 eggs
2 cups honey
1 cup coconut oil
1 ½ tsp. salt
2 ½ tsp. baking soda

1 Tbsp. vanilla (a little extra vanilla NEVER hurts!)
4 cups almond flour
1½-1¾ cups gluten-free flour (Namaste is best!)
1½ cups chopped walnuts or pecans

Mix together wet ingredients in a bowl, then add all dry ingredients. Mix until well combined and spoon into 2 parchment-lined bread pans until pans are ⅔ full. Put leftover batter in a small, greased cake pan, bake the loaves at 350°F for about 1 hour, and bake the cake for about 30 minutes until the middle of the top bounces gently back. If the cake doesn't bounce back, bake it for 5-8 minutes and test it again.

Makes 2 regular loaves and a small cake to munch on. It freezes very nicely. VERY yummy banana cake or bread! Also delicious with cream cheese frosting and if you want to be really naughty, sprinkle the frosted loaf or cake with chocolate toffee bits. Oh my, my!

Cream Cheese Frosting

Ingredients:

8 oz. softened cream cheese
½ cup softened butter
4 cups powdered sugar
2 tsp. vanilla, plus a pinch of salt

Mix all ingredients with an electric mixer until light and fluffy. Frost cooled banana cake as desired. Eat and enjoy. Add the toffee bits and enjoy even more!

Dedicated to my parents,
who took on the adventure and gift
of farming while raising their children.
They blessed our family and many, many others.

Text & Illustrations © Maryan J. Peterson
All rights reserved.

No part of this book may be reproduced or transmitted in any form or by any means without written permission from the publisher, except for brief excerpts used in literary reviews, educational settings, and social media, all of which have the author and illustrator credited and allow the book to be presented and promoted in a positive manner.

ISBN 13: 978-1-7923-7623-8

Published by Magpie Press
Cover design and typesetting by Kaitlin Barwick